GW01158180

Golden Enlightenment
2014

A Beginners Handbook for Seekers of
Spiritual Knowledge, Truth and Wisdom

James McQuitty

Other recent titles by James McQuitty

Christianity: The Sad and Shameful Truth

The Complete Guide to Spiritual Astro-Numerology

Help Yourself to a Better Life

How Psychics and Mediums Work, The Spirit and the Aura

Know Yourself

The Reason Why You Were Born

The Wisdom Oracle

Where I use the words *should* or *must* in this book it is
purely for convenience and is not intended to be a
dogmatic statement. I recognise and appreciate the
fact that we each have freewill and, ultimately, are
responsible to no one but ourselves.

www.jamesmcquitty.com

Contents

Continued...

Chapter Four - Religious

Chapter Five - Spiritual

Chapter Six – Odds & Curios

Chapter Seven – Opening the Mind

Recommended Reading

Foreword

By the Author

The original version of *Golden Enlightenment* was published twenty years ago, in 1994. Essentially, although not always using identical wording, this edition contains the same thirty-five questions with updated answers to reflect my current expression.

The intention behind this book, like the earlier version, is to provide readers with easy to follow answers to the sort of questions that most people ask when they first embark upon the quest for spiritual knowledge, truth and wisdom.

Over the many years since I began my own investigations I have found many answers, expressed in a variety of ways. Some answers have seemed quite simple to understand, and some, initially, rather complicated. Yet they all lead to the same underlying truth, that the Power we call God (or the Great Spirit, the Creator, etc) is the Source of all life, and that everyone and everything is interrelated and eternally linked.

The passing called "death" is merely a stepping forward onto another plane of eternal life.

As you read this book I hope that you will find the truth and understanding that you seek, and that this will shine a light and reveal to you a brighter pathway to follow.

If you do seek further insight into the spiritual realities of life I sincerely believe that ultimately you will pleased that you did so. I say this because in many ways it is a never-ending journey of discovery that can only inspire and uplift seekers to live a more fulfilling and purposeful life with an inner certainty in their future.

May love always go with you, and shine in your heart.

Chapter One

Survival

Questions 1 – 5

---

1. Will I Survive Death?

You can do no other than survive the passing we call death because first and foremost you *are* a spirit being.

You are not a physical being who will acquire a spirit or soul upon passing; you were already a spirit being *before* you were born.

Spirit is the power that motivates you, your energy. Your soul is your individuality that makes you unique. Both are indestructible. Mind and consciousness are part and parcel of your soul so can never perish.

Your physical form serves a purpose; it provides you - your soul - with an opportunity to experience at the physical level of being. This presents you with the opportunity to experience contrasts, the light and the dark, the positive and the negative and, as we might term them, good and bad, or right and wrong. These experiences cannot be encountered in the higher life of the spirit realms, where all is of light and at harmony at each level.

You therefore come to a world such as this earth and inhabit a limited physical form to gather greater awareness and wisdom through the myriad of experiences that life presents to everyone.

When the time comes to exit, to the soul it is like an actor finishing a role before returning to their true home. On earth we are also like the dreamer who has yet to awaken.

2. When I pass to the spirit world, will I be reunited with my loved ones?

When you pass into the spirit world you will not only be reunited with your loved ones, it is likely they will come to meet you.

You are of course an infinite spirit here and now, even though you currently function through your physical body. Since you are spirit, you cannot be truly separated from your loved ones. It is most likely that you have met them on many occasions during the sleep state, when your spirit is able to leave your physical body. This is basically the same process as 'death,' except that during 'out-of-body' sleep experiences an energy link is maintained with your physical body, keeping it alive, and allowing your spirit to return.

Your brain, being a physical organ, is unfortunately unable to remember much, if any, of your sleep state meetings. Sometimes a small fleeting recollection may register, and you may think of this as just a dream, but it is often the fragmented memories of actual experiences. Although these can become clouded as they intermingle with other data that is passing through your subconscious mind.

So, to be clear, the answer to this question is "yes" you will be reunited with your loved ones if this is something you and they wish. However, there is one proviso, and that is if you and they gravitate to the same level – which in most cases is quite likely, provided one has lived a reasonably 'good' and decent life and not to any major degree transgressed any natural spiritual laws. Basically, if you and they have lived what we might conceive of as an 'average' life, you will undoubtedly be reunited. Furthermore, even if one finds themselves at a higher level than another, they can still visit, so have no concerns over this question.

3. Do children grow-up in the spirit world?

All life continues after 'death,' regardless of the age at the time of passing. So when a child or a baby of any age, even a miscarried or aborted child, passes from the physical, spirit life and development continues.

In the spirit world there are places of rest, and of learning, along with all the care and attention that any individual could possibly need. So happiness is assured for all children.

Spirit growth is not the same as physical growth. As we age upon earth our bodies reflect this, it is natural. If all is well physical form, like a flower, grows to maturity and when passed its peak gradually fades and eventually 'dies.' Whereas growth in spirit is in consciousness, we gradually evolve to express ourselves on higher and higher levels of spirit life.

However, initially upon passing we remain much as we were upon earth. The bodies we manifest for ourselves are a reflection of how we think. So a child will to all intents and purposes still appear as and be a child even if they are an experienced 'older' soul. Initially they will still think as a child, and will be pleased to visit those loved ones they remember upon earth. This is why messages that may be passed through a medium will say that such and such a child is communicating with a parent, for instance.

Time in spirit life passes quicker than linear time does on earth. What to us may seem ten or twenty, even fifty long years, to the one who has gone ahead may speed past in a comparative flash. The higher the level of spirit life the speedier time seems to fly.

So to answer this question clearly, it is "yes" children do effectively grow-up in spirit life. As time passes the soul can effectively 'picture' itself and therefore manifest at a peak age rather than as a child and appear and communicate with a 'grown' appearance when described by a medium.

4. What happens to suicides?

Whenever possible those who commit suicide will be met and cared for in the same way that all can be guided and helped. There is no damnation or eternal punishment awaiting anyone.

It is quite usual for a loved one, a relative or friend, to meet the passing soul, to care for them and guide them on their journey home. Otherwise it will be a spirit guide or helper who will assist them. Either way they will be comforted and treated with sympathy, compassion and encouragement.

It is quite likely that first they will be guided to a place of healing, for these do exist in the spirit realms. They are needed because we can become very entrenched in the thinking processes of earthly life. It is even possible for some passing souls, who have perhaps been traumatised, to effectively put themselves into a dreamlike-coma. Gradually, the healing in spirit will help them reawaken and come to terms with what happened to them and to their 'new' status.

The act of suicide, although it draws no punishment, is one that most who experience it later regret. This is because life on earth is effectively a 'gift' and something precious and to be valued. To terminate it before its natural conclusion is by spirit people regarded as a wasted opportunity. This is because we come into physical form to become more enlightened beings through our earthly experiences. So when back in spirit, in time, we realise that we may need to try once more to face whatever it was that we avoided previously.

5. Do animals survive death?

All life continues after 'death.' Therefore, if you have lost a pet or companion animal with which you built a bond of love you will, upon your own passing, find that they have survived their own transition.

In the meantime he or she will be cared for and looked after either by one of your friends or relatives who will have recognised your mutual love, or by one of the many in the spirit world who engage themselves in the task of caring for such animals.

Wild or herd animals share what is often called a "group soul" and like our domestic friends their consciousness continues after their physical demise. But unlike our cats and dogs and other animals that have shared the love of human contact, they have no reason or desire to await or look for human companionship. Although at some point in the future their day for this to dawn will undoubtedly arrive.

As I said in answer three, time in spirit life passes quicker than linear time does on earth. So our former pets or companions hardly notice what to us may prove many years, even decades, before we reunite with them. Then, when we are brought into contact they are able to resume their lives with us as though apart for the briefest of times.

We are able to continue this rekindled relationship for as long as it suits us to do so. Although eventually, and this may be in what we would count hundreds of years, we may deem it appropriate to move aside and allow our friend or friends an open pathway to pursue their own spirit progression. No doubt a sense of 'knowing when the time is right' will then come to us, as we will be using our heightened spirit senses with total honesty and integrity.

All life is in progression from the lower to the higher – but there is no rush.

Chapter Two

Personal & Philosophical

Questions 6 – 11

---

6. If I have married twice, after my death, will I have to choose between my former partners?

Life in the spirit world is rather different from life upon earth. In a sense there are still 'rules,' things you can or cannot do. But these 'rules' are universal or natural laws, not earth-made rules. They could also be considered as the laws of the Great Spirit in operation.

Over the centuries upon earth many ideas of how life should be organised, controlled and ruled have been instigated. All of these, including marriage, are earthly judgements which have no bearing or consequence in the spirit world. This is because contracts or vows, written or verbal, cease at passing.

Life in the spirit world is in harmonious accord with the natural laws of the Great Spirit. Love in the spirit world is a matter of natural attraction in its purest sense. Upon earth, as I am sure you are aware, attraction can be of a more superficial nature.

If you have had two, three or many more marriage partners it would not be of importance to anyone in the spirit world. You are free to be with whichever partner you choose, provided your attraction and desire is reciprocated. Or, if you so choose, you do not have to be with either or any partner because each of us is a free spirit with total freedom of choice.

7. Why was I born?

You, like everyone else, chose to be born in order to "learn lessons" as they are called, through your physical experiences.

Each physical lifetime teaches a little more, until finally you will reach the level where you no longer need to return to earth. Although even at this stage of attainment you can still choose to be return, in order to serve as a teacher, or a healer, for the guidance and benefit of others.

There are many 'lessons' to encounter, they are encased in the everyday experiences that allow us the opportunity to behave or react in a kind and loving way. The lessons embrace aspects of charity, compassion, courage, dedication, faith, forgiveness, generosity, honesty, kindness, patience, responsibility, self-love, and ultimately unconditional love. As we learn to follow and express the inner qualities of the soul we progress as more enlightened spirit beings.

As we progress the vibrations of the soul quicken (are raised to a higher and faster rate) so that we can progress to higher levels of spirit life and expression.

This, generally speaking, is the reason why you were born, although in each lifetime we may be attempting to learn just one or a few aspects. Each time we will deliberately attempt to encounter some aspect we have not garnered previously, or have perhaps struggled to take on board in the 'right' way.

Earth life, as we all know, can be very challenging –
which is why we choose it, because the greater the
challenge we face, the greater the progress that can
be forthcoming – if we respond how the soul would
wish.

8. Does it matter how I live my life, since I will survive anyway?

How you live your life is of great importance, not only
can it have an effect upon your present day-to-day
life, but it can also impact upon your long-term spirit
future.

Ideally, you should strive to live in harmony with the
yearnings of your own spirit, while duly respecting
others. To do so, I suggest you use your inner
feelings from the heart, or your conscience and
intuition, and allow these feelings to be your guide.

You should recognise that the universal law of cause
and effect is forever in operation. This, in more
biblical language guarantees that "as you sow, so
shall you reap." Or in modern terms, "what goes

around comes around," or what you give you get back.

What this all means is that through the natural outworking of the law whatever you do in this lifetime will have repercussions that will affect your future. Results can be forthcoming during this lifetime, they can also prove a factor in the level you find yourself on when you pass, and they may also need to be redressed in some way in a future incarnation.

Spirit teachings do not try to scare people or 'bring them into line' to behave as obedient sheep. We are 'free agents' at all times. What they endeavour to do is open our eyes to the truth, and the facts of how the spiritual universe works. This allows us the opportunity to make an informed choice or decision based on genuine knowledge.

Typically, spirit communicators bring love, laughter and upliftment with no judgement. If we can emulate this I think we will be doing well.

9. Can anything to be gained by understanding survival of death, and by the study of spirit teachings?

By understanding the factual truth of survival after 'death,' and the knowledge that spirit teachings bring of eternal life and natural laws, you should feel more encouraged to question every action of your life; thus potentially enhancing your spiritual growth and progression.

One way in which you can gain is by learning to judge yourself and your motives in all you think, say and do. Even an elementary study of spirit teachings gives the seeker the realisation that there is no escape from the consequences of one's own making. Therefore, this gives you the opportunity to become a more spiritually enlightened being, and the chance to make far greater advances in your spiritual progression than might have been the case if you lacked this knowledge.

10. Is every action of my life planned, or can freewill change what would otherwise be my destiny?

You, everyone, is born with what is called a "life plan." It is a plan that you would have agreed to in the spirit realms before your birth. It is planned in such a way to give you the opportunities to experience lessons that will assist the further advancement of your soul.

Obviously, it is a plan that you should wish to co-operate with, as in the long run this will give you the greatest progress. However, this is easier said than done, as you do not remember the plan whilst on earth. There are good reasons for this. One is because if we consciously remembered the plan we might change our minds; secondly, if we consciously followed the plan we would lack spontaneity and the impact of any "lesson" would be devalued.

This may sound rather bizarre, but would you, for instance, take a pathway that you knew was going to lead to any form of suffering (physical, emotional or mental) if in advance you realised where it would lead? I doubt that I would. Yet in the fullness of time most of us can look back at certain events in our lives and say, "it wasn't nice at the time, but I did learn from it." Generally, we become a better person.

We have freewill on earth and this can of course cause havoc. Life-plans are not always followed; our soul may try to nudge us in the right direct, as might our guides, but sometimes the pleasure and pursuits of the earthplane prove too great a distraction and we take what spiritually speaking is a less than desirable path.

However, since life-plans enable us to learn from the impact of experiences, how we cope and react and so forth, the precise physical details can sometimes be adjusted to still allow the lesson to be encountered. So what we miss one day, week or year, will often repeat in a similar fashion so that you learn equally as well as you would have done if you had taken the first planned route.

11. Will I be judged when I die, and if so by whom?

Upon your 'death' *you* will be sole judge, although, natural law will determine the level to which you aspire.

In the fullness of time, to assist your understanding and to degree evaluation, you will be shown what will effectively be a replay of your entire life (all the significant points). You will judge or assess, with feelings of happiness and delight accompanying good and more pleasing moments and no doubt with sadness when you review moments of regret.

You should therefore have no fear of any 'day of judgement' with entry into heaven or hell as the reward or the sentence. However, at the same time, you should consider that as your own judge you are likely to be very critical, and the ego cannot hide the truth. In spirit life the truth of the kind of soul we are, and the progress made, is carried for all to see in the very vibrations that are visible to all.

Others will not judge you, but your vibrations will indicate your level of attainment and therefore, as I have said, natural law will determine the realm to which you will gravitate.

The "life-review" that all souls experience will also help you to realise which 'lessons' you have absorbed adequately and which you may need to encounter or make a further attempt at assimilating in a future incarnation.

Chapter Three

Suffering

Questions 12 - 15

---

12. If the Great Spirit is all seeing and all knowing, why is so much suffering permitted in this world?

The omnipresent consciousness - *The Great Spirit*, does not limit your spiritual growth by decreeing which lessons are available to you, allowing you the pleasure of one, while shielding you from another because it is painful. If this was so, you would not develop with a complete or balanced understanding, and your spiritual progression and attainment would be limited.

The Great Spirit has given you freewill and personal responsibility for all that you say, do and think. This gives you the choice of how, when and where you undertake to experience the many and varied lessons of life. Suffering might, on a higher level of consciousness and for specific reason be chosen, although it is just as likely to be the consequences of your own past actions, diet or negative thinking, for example, or the result of circumstances or events caused by others. The Great Spirit interferes in no one's freewill.

13. Why are some people born with physical or mental challenges?

There could be several reasons why someone might be born into a physical body that is imperfect in some way. One possible reason, as mentioned in the previous answer, is that such a life was chosen on a higher level of consciousness before birth; the soul makes the choice so that they can experience and learn from the difficulties that such an incarnation bring.

As you might imagine, not everyone can be neatly fitted into a category of "predetermined before birth." Accidents, errors of judgement, by others present on earth before one's birth do sometimes occur. For example, the medical profession do sometimes make mistakes.

Yet even then the soul of the child will likely have chosen to accept the challenge, and the life-plan adjusted to fit the circumstances.

The parents of a child born under such circumstances naturally consider it a tragedy. Yet they often rise to the challenge of being a carer and inspirer to the child, and each soul touched is able to advance through the experiences.

14. Why do some people have an easier life than others?

Before birth you will have co-operated with more advanced spirit advisors to develop a life-plan designed to enable you to learn and spiritually advance through the experiences you encounter.

The precision of this plan can be quite detailed and would have included knowledge of your intended parents - right down to the name you would be given. Even the date of your birth may have been calculated to attract certain astrological influences (vibrations).

Most importantly, your plan is for certain personal experiences or lessons that pertain to your needs. These are to be undertaken for your own benefit and quite possibly to assist others too. It is all about spiritual growth and progression. It is seldom desirable to incarnate into what we might, whilst using our earthly consciousness, consider an idyllic life-style.

It might help if you think of yourself as an actor, one who has accepted a role that you deem ideal for you at this particular stage of your career. You are appearing in a very realistic play titled "a lifetime upon earth."

Some may chose or accept a simple part, playing an average person, while others are just right for the seemingly star role of hero or martyr. In this incarnation you play one role, and perhaps next time around you will play a completely different one. In the grand scheme of things, all will eventually balance fairly and you will have played all the parts necessary to complete a full and comprehensive program of learning; then perhaps you can take on the role of the director (a spirit guide to others).

15. What can be said to comfort the bereaved?

It can be very difficult to know what to say to those bereaved because every person is an individual, and will therefore react and respond in a different way.

Whatever you say ought to be with great care and tenderness, gently expressing concern for their feelings. However, from a spiritual teaching perspective the truth, as you understand it, should be introduce them. If they already have awareness and knowledge of spiritual teachings, they should hopefully be in a better position to come to terms with their loss. But just because they have spiritual understanding, does not necessarily make the loss easy to bear, as they will miss, and grieve for the physical presence.

If they have some spirit knowledge you can slowly and gently remind them of it. Talking of the beautiful and harmonious place that their loved one will now inhabit, and of how they are probably looking down, and wondering what all the fuss is about.

If they do not have any spiritual knowledge, the same gentle expression of the truth can be introduced to them. You can also slowly add more information, bringing them more comfort, understanding, and peace of mind.

The first point that will probably concern them is whether the departed one is still truly alive, and then whether they are all right and happy, in their new life and world. You can therefore explain the truth of life after physical death, and that nobody ever truly dies. That if their loved one suffered any pain they will now be free of all such suffering. If they had any physical problems, they are also now behind them. You can explain that the body they now use, their spirit body, is a perfect one, full of health, life, vigour and strength.

You can add that where they will now live, there is no hunger or thirst, no cold winters, and no reason for sadness. They are now in a world where they can see and understand the true nature of life. They no longer have anything to worry them or cause fear.

Their new quality of life will be second to none, in a perfect, friendly, harmonious, loving land of pure delight.

You can continue to say that the departed one would have been met by relatives or friends that were already in the spirit world. Also that if the departed one had previously mourned the passing of another, that they would now be reunited. Furthermore if they had loved a pet (or companion) animal that passed before them, you can tell of how the animals survive, and of how they would also have been waiting for them.

You can go on to say that the departed one will be able to visit them, and will be much happier to see them continuing with their life in a cheerful manner. That if when they visit they see them sad, it will sadden them. For they are now in a world in which they can express themselves in all manner of ways, with no financial or other restrictions, that might have prevented such expression upon earth.

You can also point out the good news - that since we are all here to learn lessons, then the departed one more than likely learnt all that they came to learn, and was therefore free, and happy to return to the true home, the spirit world.

So do not mourn their loss – celebrate their life, whether it was short or many in earthly years.

Chapter Four

Religious

Questions 16 - 20

---

16. Why do various religions insist on the blind dogma of their own faith, suppressing their followers from seeking their own truth?

Through their spiritual nature, when this has been allowed to shine through, people have always intuitively known that life was more than just a physical experience. Within the very fabric of the soul is a desire to progress. However, during the development of the current world religions, and herein I am principally referring to Christianity, the lower nature, encompassing greed, self-interest and material desires, gained control.

The corrupt of earlier times quickly realised the power that was available to them by taking charge of religion. They were able to direct it as they saw fit and to favour themselves. Early religion was also tied-in with the law, so to object to any decision was to put one's life in jeopardy. Even today it is still the case in certain countries.

Power corrupts, and the lower nature is easily corrupted. While those with power do not give it up easily. Those who suppress and insist on others following their faith and laws do so to keep themselves powerful, many follow blindly, knowing no other way of life.

The Church discourage personal investigation by instilling fear, suggesting that anyone who does attempt to investigate may inadvertently become involved in some form of evil. They use this fear as a means of control. Although it is more often the case that those in authority in the Church have never themselves investigated and therefore can have no way of judging whether something is true or false.

All good teachers agree that to seek is to find.

17. It is said that we are created in the image of God, what does this mean?

This is a true statement in the sense that it is the spirit that is a reflection or an aspect of God. All spirit, all life, emanates from the Power we call God.

Therefore a flower or a tree is also an aspect of God, as are the birds and the bees, and all in nature. God is the motivating force behind and within all life; nothing exists separate from God.

This wonderful eternal force is within and a part of you and can never be extinguished. So you are a miniature version of God, and have the possibilities within you to grow and reach god-like heights; to be as and at one with God. This is your ultimate aim and the journey although an eternal one is a great and inspirational climb.

18. Is there a heaven and a hell?

What is called heaven exists in a higher vibrational state of existence. It is another dimension that is also, amongst other names, called the spirit world.

Within the spirit world many realms or spheres of existence exist. These realms or spheres are levels or divisions between various rates of vibration, the higher the frequency or rate of vibration, the greater the level of progress made by the spirits that live there.

As you progress, in spirit life and through many incarnations, you will gradually move up these levels, as the more you evolve spiritually the faster your own soul energies will vibrate, and you will naturally be drawn to the level that matches your own progression.

The earthplane vibrates at a comparatively slow rate of vibration. The varying frequencies from the lowly earth to the highly progressed states of spirit life are easy to describe as high or low. However, this is rather a misleading description as in reality it is really faster and slower. The terminology of higher and lower, gives the impression of a heaven above or higher, and therefore the potential for a hell below.

As for hell, well no such literal place exists, not in the sense of a place where spirits are tortured or chained up in a burning furnace or cave. However, there are lower levels, existing on slower vibrational spheres. These spheres are definitely to be avoided (by living a decent respectful life), but nobody is trapped there forever. Progress is open to those who inhabit such realms, allowing them to learn, show remorse and make recompense if necessary, and gradually move up to higher levels.

The higher the level, the nicer it reportedly is.

There are of course people on earth who are far from any reasonable person's definition of good. Some inflict on others a life that is very much a depiction of a hell upon earth. When any soul who has mistreated others leave their physical body for the last time they can quite easily find themselves drawn to an undesirable level of existence.

It is also possible for some souls to attach themselves to the earthplane, to become "earthbound." They can be attracted to those upon the earth with similar thoughts and desires, for it is a universal law that "like attracts like." But this is extremely rare, and is not something that anyone should pay too much attention to or in any way fear. The higher your own thoughts, the higher your vibrations, and you will have a certain amount of natural protection from any undesired attractions.

If you think good thoughts, and live a good life, you will attract good influences around you, good guides and helpers. They in turn will try to help you in your progress, and when your time comes to return to the spirit world, you will find yourself being guided to a wonderful place.

19. What is sin?

One definition of sin is to behave, by thought, word, or action, in a way that is contradictory to your own soul. This, in turn, is inharmonious with the natural laws of God.

People seem to have lived with the guilt of sin for many centuries. In my experience sin is never mentioned by communicators from the spirit world. Often, what people are told is sinful is used as a threat by the clergy who masquerade as intermediaries of God.

It is a sin against oneself when your thoughts, words and actions are in contradiction to your own soul. Your higher self knows when you are taking the wrong path, or thinking in a way that is unbecoming of the soul you are. Natural laws guarantee that we will learn by our own mistakes, and over many incarnations when necessary.

When we live inharmoniously to our own soul or higher consciousness direction this can cause disruption to the subtle bodies (the aura) and this can lead to health problems or disease. Naturally, this is not a good idea. But no 'sin' leads to punishment from God. Repercussions come entirely by way of natural laws. Natural laws help to educate and teach the soul and in time bring order, balance and harmony.

Naturally, murder, or inflicting pain and suffering in any callous or deliberate way will carry negative repercussions to the soul of the perpetrator. This includes the probability of finding oneself on an undesirable level upon passing, so should never be contemplated.

Yet, in the fullness of time, even those actions that can easily be labelled "sinful" remain more a sin against oneself. I say this because, at a soul level, the innocent parties, although they may be in need of healing, carry no negative repercussions into their spirit life. While those who perpetrated 'sinful' actions upon others will have to face the consequences of their actions.

20. Was Jesus divine or simply a great medium and healer?

Jesus, like all of us, was and is divine; for we are all aspects of God, and as such are divine. Jesus, like Buddha, Krishna, and many others, came to teach people that life is eternal, and that God is the father (creator) of all.

Jesus the man, whilst upon earth, would have had to work on himself, in the same way that all people do. It is unlikely that he was born with, or awoke one day, and knew 'all' answers.

Though, it does seem that he was a natural medium with excellent clairvoyance and clairaudience. He must also have been a marvellous channel for healing energies. He should be remembered as a great teacher and a highly spiritual soul.

The final outcome of his physical life appears to be one that he could have avoided; instead he used the opportunity to return after 'death,' as final and conclusive proof of survival, for the benefit of his disciples and followers.

The soul that incarnated as "Jesus" reportedly resides at a very advanced level of spirit life, and is a member of what is termed the "spirit hierarchy." Those at this level help to oversee many of us below. It is a level where the highest compassion and love are attributes fully embraced within their souls.

Chapter Five

Spiritual

Questions 21 - 30

---

21. Why do some people fear spirit communication and knowledge?

Ignorance is undoubtedly the reason for the fear many people hold for what they consider, "the unknown." They have some vague belief in life after 'death' but are opposed to spirit communication because they mistakenly believe this disturbs the so-called dead. They sometimes believe the 'dead' have gone to a place of rest, to wait a day of judgement and should not be disturbed until that day comes. They do not understand that the 'dead' cannot be disturbed, because they have never truly died.

When they communicate, directly or more commonly through mediums upon earth, spirits are not being 'disturbed' or 'called-up,' they return because they wish to do so. Always it is the spirits who initiate communication, which is not possible without their desire to co-operate; for no medium can guarantee who will communicate. It is entirely the choice of those from the spirit world.

Many people who are fearful, perhaps without realising why, do not want the responsibility that genuine spiritual knowledge and truth can bring. This is because the discovery of spiritual truths does indeed bring responsibility.

Once you recognise the truth you can no longer blame fate or God for your good or bad fortune. Spiritual knowledge teaches you that every action and consequence of your life is of your own making, your personal responsibility.

Indeed, it is possible that you are now reaping according to how you have sown in a past life. Understanding spiritual truths and laws gives you the opportunity to take command of your life with a completely different and more positive outlook.

22. Psychics, clairvoyants and mediums, what is the difference?

Around you there is an aura, a vibrating energy field which constantly changes according to how you think and what you do. Effectively, it is an instantly updated reflection of you. It shows the current state of your health, emotional and mental advancement or concerns, and your spiritual development or growth, and much more.

When you touch or hold an object your energy vibrations can be temporarily transmitted to them, as well as to the clothing or jewellery you wear. Something that you are in regular or constant contact with will absorb a stronger or longer lasting vibration. A psychic is able, through contact with your aura, or an object that you touch or wear, to attune through their own vibrational and auric senses, to your vibrations, and gain feelings about you. We all have the ability to receive such vibrational information, but not all of us are able to attune our sensitivity to the correct level. Psychics are able to attune themselves and interpret these vibrations, but need not call on any link being made with the spirit world. They may not in fact be able to consciously link with the spirit world.

A medium however, is a person who is able to attune themselves with those from the spirit world. We are all spirit as well as physical beings whilst upon the earth, and it should therefore come as no surprise to find some amongst us who are able to communicate, spirit to spirit. The difficult part comes in the translation of the communication to the physical consciousness of the medium. This has to be sufficient so that it can be understood and passed as a message to the person for whom it is intended.

One of these methods is called clairvoyance. A clairvoyant is able to receive communication, in the form of pictures, in much the same way that you may receive pictures when you sleep and dream. The pictures a clairvoyant receives are usually very clear and strong impressions, the impressions often giving a clue to their meaning. A developing clairvoyant will build up their own interpretation of what they receive, thus one picture or scene will generally always mean the same thing to them, enabling them to give an accurate interpretation.

Another form of mediumship is clairaudience. A clairaudient is able to hear spirit communications. The finer channels in this form of mediumship are able to pass messages word for word, which can prove very accurate and detailed.

A third way some mediums receive communication is referred to as clairsentience, to actually feel impressions upon their body, such as if the communicator had trouble breathing, near the end of their physical life, the same feeling can be temporarily given, or transferred to the medium.

Many mediums are able to receive communication combining two or all three of these forms of mediumship, making the message that they are receiving and giving all the more detailed and accurate.

Mediums, like people in all trades, can vary greatly between highly accurate and accomplished to those less sensitive and, consequently, less accurate. Although, I am sure all genuine mediums do their best, but like all of us, are only human.

23. Is reincarnation a fact and if so, do I have to reincarnate?

You (that is your "soul") is likely to have experienced many physical incarnations upon the earth. This is because the life lessons of earth are too varied, and many, to experience in just one incarnation. So in order to learn all of the lessons that can be experienced whilst in a physical body, and are necessary for spiritual growth, returning many times is quite normal.

Each time it is with a plan, with the lessons and experiences that we intend to encounter aimed to produce greater spiritual growth. At a soul level, every proceeding life adds to the knowledge of the previous life. This process continues until all the necessary lessons that you can learn upon earth have been absorbed.

Gender is of no major relevance to the soul, so it is quite normal to swap between male and female during various lifetimes, if this will enable the soul to experience what it needs.

The opportunity to reincarnate is a blessing, no one is compelled to return against their will, it is seen as a chance to try again, to improve, and to spiritually grow all the more. Indeed, spiritual growth is the single most important reason for your life on earth.

Eventually you *will* reach the level of knowledge and wisdom which will free you from any *need* to return, but even when this time comes you may choose to return, to help others.

In that higher state of spirit life you recognise the valuable lessons that the higher you (your soul) has learnt, through your experiences upon the earth.

When life becomes uncomfortable upon earth the thought of returning seems unattractive. But when you return to the spirit world and a true understanding of eternity awakens within you, this will enable you to put the time span of a physical incarnation into perspective, to realise that in eternity it is really very brief. So when all is ready, which might be many years of our time, you will undoubtedly once again choose to continue your lessons and seek to experience another physical lifetime. Remember, you chose or accepted your current incarnation.

24. If I have lived previously, why do I not remember doing so?

At present your consciousness is experiencing through the senses of your physical body that function through your brain. Your physical brain is a new organ appertaining to your current body; it played no part in any previous lifetime, and was not present during any time spent in the spirit world. It therefore can only know what it has experienced in your current life.

To remember any aspects of a previous life you would have to raise your consciousness to a much higher level. This is sometimes achievable during meditation, or can be accessed whilst sleeping (when we can temporarily leave the physical body and visit the spirit world) and recalled as dreams, but is likely to come as fleeting recollections or flash backs, making it very difficult to identify in any certain way.

Many people have also accessed information whilst under hypnotic trance, but here it is difficult to be certain that the subconscious is not indulging itself, or that the mind is not linking-in to the experiences of someone else. Although it has been fairly well established that in many cases the information received under hypnosis is from a personal, previous incarnation (appertaining to the soul). The proof is often reflected in fears and phobias of the current life being caused by actual events of a previous incarnation. For example, death by drowning in a previous incarnation can lead to an irrational fear or phobia of water in the current life.

But without hypnosis, it is generally rare to obtain memories of a past life, as the memories do not usually have any purpose to fulfil in your current life. Sometimes memories could actually be a burden in your current life. It would be very uncomfortable to intimately remember being a man if now a women or vice-versa. It could also be like going to school knowing some of the answers, devaluing the lessons planned for this lifetime. It is therefore part of the plan that you do not generally remember, or have access to certain memories, unless they need to be released, such as in the cases of carried over fears which have caused phobias.

All valued memories are retained within the soul mind, which is eternal. The physical brain, which obviously perishes at 'death,' during its lifespan has limited access to the spirit mind, although it is influenced by it through conscience, intuition and other guiding or inspirational thoughts during earth life.

25. Is there such a thing as good karma?

What can be called "Good karma" is created. Whenever you show compassion, are kind and forgiving, you help others and reveal your inner love through your actions, your soul must reap the positive effect. Your "reward" will be the advancement of your soul.

Everything you do, say and think in life has an effect, not just upon others, but also upon your soul. Furthermore, like attracts like, and as well as drawing to you those of a like mind on earth, this extends out to people from the spirit side of life.

What we would consider good people draw equally good spirit souls. The artist on earth draws those from the spirit realms who also love art, and they may try to be of some assistance. On the negative side of the coin, those who are sadly living a destructive life in some form will attract to them those who in their lifetime were of a like mind.

So it is worth your while developing a positive attitude, as well as leading a life that will be beneficial to your soul. Karma is an eternal process, and even if you do not seem to receive rewards in your current incarnation, you will do so in the spirit world or in a future incarnation.

Another point that is worth consideration is that your creation of good karma also helps to raise the consciousness of the whole of creation. As in a broader sense the whole of creation is one, having all come from the same divine source, from God.

26. What is the difference between spirit guides and guardian angels and what is the angelic kingdom?

During the course of your physical life, many spirit world people will take an interest in you. Some will be relatives that have gone ahead, and are still concerned or interested in your progress. Others will include those with a similar personality to yourself, who wish to either help you, or perhaps to learn with you. Also you may have old friends from this incarnation, and even from passed incarnations.

But nearest to you always, are your guide and your guardian angel. Your main guide has agreed to stay with, or close to you, throughout your current incarnation. There are also other guides, teachers, who come and go from time to time. Your guide will try to help you during your present incarnation, and all the more so during more testing periods of time. He can help you in many ways, for example, by attempting to influence your moods, by bringing a feeling of peace and calm to you during stressful moments. Also by bringing upliftment when you are feeling down. He can also transfer impressions and ideas to your mind and in this way help to guide you, with great care and compassion.

You may think that all this sounds rather unlikely, and that you never receive such help. But as an example, you need only look at the many novelists, comedy and song writers, who talk of how ideas just pop into their minds. Many also receive inspiration during their sleep state, in the form of lucid dreams. Everyone receives help to some degree, throughout their entire physical life, but often it may seem so natural, that they do not realise it.

You may think that when you have an idea or a thought that you were not consciously trying to cultivate, that it is merely the workings of your own subconscious mind. With information coming to the surface from past memories of things you may have heard or read. This may on occasions be the case, but often it is your guide trying to help you, although he is not always able to do so simply because you will have to go through certain experiences which you accepted before birth, in order to learn from them, and thus develop and grow spiritually.

You also have your own freewill, and although your guide may succeed in directing an idea to formulate in your mind, whether you choose to follow or reject the idea is your own decision.

In a similar way your guardian angel, who will remain with you until your passing, is also trying to help your spiritual growth.

Your guardian angel is from a different line of evolution from your guide, and from yourself. Your guide is a human spirit, and will probably have lived many incarnations upon the earth. Your guardian angel is from the angelic kingdom of evolution, and is unlikely to have ever experienced a physical incarnation upon the earth. Although it is said that angels have assisted in the evolution of life on earth since its very beginning.

The angelic kingdom is truly wonderful, they come willingly to help people, animals and nature. There are many angels, other than guardian angels, who serve in all manner of ways, such as angels who direct energies during healing services, or whenever a prayer reaches them.

Under the direction of the angels, and also under the angelic kingdom, are many lines of creation, there are nature spirits, such as fairies and gnomes. There are also elemental spirits, who exist within such as minerals, stones and crystals. All of creation has life, and is assisted by life, in forms that are almost beyond our imagination and comprehension in their complexity and numbers.

Every single flower, plant and tree is attended by nature spirits who take to them vital life energy forces, without which they would cease to grow and develop. The very colour and scent of a flower is said to be there only because of the work of nature spirits.

There are nature spirits that exist in the four elements of earth, air, fire and water, each serving and working with purpose, to sustain and develop life. Most of these nature spirits can reportedly change size at will, and will do so depending upon the task at hand. You cannot see these wonderful manifestations of angelic love unless you possess well developed clairvoyant vision, as they are etheric (spirit energy) in nature, and so cannot be seen by the physical eye.

If people were to co-operate with the nature spirits the response in nature would be significant. Crops should be grown without artificial or chemical fertilisers and pesticides, which the nature spirits dislike. Then, through prayer, by asking the nature spirits to help the growth and development of the crops, much bigger and healthier yields would be forthcoming.

The nature spirits desire nothing more than to be of service and to work harmoniously with people, and given the chance, and the right circumstances, would do so to a much greater affect than circumstances permit at present.

Crops organically grown in this way taste better, but perhaps even more importantly, they also have much greater life force within them, which gives much more nourishment and nutrient to the consumer.

If you are a gardener, or grow your own fruit or vegetables, you are probably already working in harmony with nature spirits, even if you are not consciously aware of doing so. But now that you are more aware, why not try praying to them, and asking them for their help, you may well be pleasantly surprised by the results you achieve.

27. Is spiritual healing beneficial?

Spiritual healing, which is a method of channelling remedial energies can be most beneficial.

When a healer prays to be used as a channel and, typically, places his or her hands close to or upon another, healing energies will flow through.

However, it does not always follow that the receiver will make a full or even a partial recovery. There are various reasons for this. Perhaps, for example, the receiver has been born with a life-plan that involves going through a certain illness or problem? If it was removed the lesson would be denied.

Naturally, not all illnesses and problems are in the nature of spiritual lessons; there are a multitude of possible reasons. The same illnesses and problems can occur if you fail to look after your physical body, remember you have freewill.

Spiritual healing can help in nearly all cases, but if the illness or problem is caused by certain behaviour or action, or even a certain thought process that continues after healing has begun, the effects of the healing will be limited or quickly fade. If, for another example, you receive healing for a strained back, and after receiving healing, you go out and start lifting heavy boxes, the result will very likely be a return to square one, if not worse. So do consider your own choice of actions, spiritual healing can and does help, but it is rare to get a miraculous or instant recovery. Responses are more often in relation to the illness or problem, and a long standing or more serious illness or problem will usually take longer to respond than a more recent or minor illness or problem.

On the other hand, if there is no lesson to be experienced and no thought or action that hinders the flow of healing energies, then benefits, even those that may appear miraculous, can result.

28. Do people in the spirit world have bodies like ours?

At what is called the "astral" level of the spirit world, which is where most people find themselves when they first pass, people do continue to use a body that seems as real and as tangible to them as your physical body is to you.

Whereas those who have progressed to higher realms have little need of the outward physical appearance to which you and I have grown accustomed. They still have a soul but this has been described as "mist-like" if at all visible to those in realms below their own status.

However, for those spirit people who have not yet reached such levels of attainment, the body they use is initially a duplicate in appearance of the physical body they used when upon earth but without any defects.

For example, if you had a physical body that was scarred, missing a limb, or with impaired vision when you passed into the spirit world, such defects would no longer exist. This is because physical defects do not affect your perfect soul body. Your soul body cannot become ill, nor can it be harmed. Furthermore, since spirit is eternal and ageless, if you pass in old age it is most common to revert to an appearance from your prime. The way that you think of yourself will become your reality. If you pass over still young, you will mature only to an appearance you are happy with and not beyond. The perfect system you might say? And why not - it is "heaven" to us.

29. Is prayer beneficial and if so how should I pray?

The power of prayer is a great and wonderful thing and should be used on a regular basis. It works best when the prayer is a sincere thought and gesture, coming from the heart. It should be used for enlightenment, guidance, healing, protection, and in many more ways, but always for a high ideal and motive.

Prayer, to be most effective, needs to be a concentrated mental projection of your thoughts.

There is no strict rule to the composition, the wording should be based upon personal experience, if it feels or sounds right, it is right for you. The words can be said in the mind, for telepathic communication is used in the spirit world (or out loud if you wish).

You can either direct your thoughts to guides, angels, or directly to God, either way they will be heard. As a simple guideline, I would suggest you go into a quiet room, relax and close your eyes, then begin, for example asking that healing should be directed or given to those you know are unwell. There is no limit, and distance is no object, finishing with a thank you.

All prayers should naturally be of good motive and with an open nature, and never seeking an outcome that is unworthy. A prayer asking for personal acquisition or financial gain, just because you might enjoy it, would seem unworthy. But a prayer for financial help for those in real genuine need, rather than a want, would be worthy. This does not mean all seemingly justified prayers will be answered in the way desired, they will be heard, and not ignored, but there might be reasons why help cannot be given, such as a karmic situation.

Of course not all apparently unanswered prayers are karmic related; there are many plans which cannot be seen from the physical perspective. Plans which interweave many people together, even for a short period of time, and what effects one might have a knock-on effect upon others, so from the physical level, it is near impossible to fully understand why many things happen or do not happen.

So please do pray, for the very act of doing so is uplifting to the soul because it acknowledges the reality of the greater life and Power.

30. Can spiritual gifts be developed?

Some people are born with what are termed natural gifts or abilities. They may see or hear spirit visitors, or perhaps possess a psychic sense of awareness, where they are able to predict an event a little in advance of its occurrence. Or they can sense that something has happened before anyone else has heard the news.

These are quite likely people that before birth decided upon a life of service, using their gift to in some way help others. They have earned the right to be born with their gift already developed to a certain degree, perhaps through the efforts of many previous incarnations.

A far greater number of people that eventually develop gifts begin life with no obvious gift. Many go half way through their life in total ignorance that they possess any sort of potential worthy of development.

All people have some potential because we are all spirit beings. But there are reasons why some will develop as better channels for communication or healing. Firstly, if you wish to develop, you must have the desire, coupled with an honourable motive. You must also display a reasonable level of commitment and dedication. Last but not least, you will need patience, and must be willing to make personal sacrifices. All of these qualities must be within you if you are to develop any potential gift.

The most recommended way to begin to unfold any potential gift is to sit in daily meditation, and where possible to join a development circle. This can be where the test of patience, commitment and dedication first come in. Many practicing mediums sat in such development circles for many years before being confidently able to demonstrate their gift.

Wise mediums often continue to sit in circles and to meditate because no matter how proficient they may appear, they can always improve themselves.

Not everyone is a potential medium, in the sense of clairvoyance, clairaudience or healing. Many people have other equally valuable gifts to share, such as the arts, music, singing, and comedy. To be able to make others laugh is indeed a wonderful and therapeutic gift. So not everyone in life will, or is intended to develop, potential mediumistic gifts, the reason being that their life plan might well be dedicated to other experiences and lessons. Although peaceful meditation will always be beneficial, nothing is ever wasted.

Chapter Six

Odds & Curios

Questions 31 - 34

---

31. Is meditation a good idea and if so, how should I meditate?

Meditation gradually brings peace to the mind, which can also help to maintain or restore harmony to the aura, and this is beneficial to health. Therefore, it is certainly a "good idea."

Meditation can be undertaken singularly or in groups, it can be in silence, with a guided talk, or with the influence of gentle, pleasant music. There are no set rules, as you must find the best format for yourself, and even this may change from time to time.

At the outset some people like to first relax their body. Various methods can be used to help you relax, such as flexing or contracting your muscles, and then releasing the tension. It helps some people if at the outset of meditation they hold a mental picture, such as the flame of a candle, or perhaps a favourite flower.

The object is to discipline the mind and aid concentration so that your thoughts do not keep wandering away onto daily activities of your everyday life.

I personally find that music aids relaxation, it also creates vibrations of colour, and can assist in self healing, as it helps to bring mind, body and spirit into greater harmony.

Lone meditation is perhaps associated with someone isolating themselves in a quiet room, sitting in a comfortable chair (some prefer an upright chair as this is better for the spine), and perhaps playing music for fifteen to thirty minutes or so. This may well be the ideal method of meditation for many people.

However, those who find meditation quite natural or are more accomplished at it can often find themselves in a meditative state almost anywhere. On a quiet seat in the park, sitting on a grass bank, or leaning against a tree. There are no rules, the peace of mind it brings may last simply for a brief moment or two, but this is fine as even the shortest of times can be therapeutic to the soul.

Meditation is not necessarily a means of unfolding or developing psychic or spiritual gifts, although this may come when and if the time is right. So do not hold fast to expectations of the development of clairvoyance or clairaudience, as this may never happen. Seek inner peace and understanding that you are one with God, and a part of the whole of creation.

32. Is positive thinking beneficial?

Your mind is more powerful than you may realise. As you think you create effects that can be positive or negative. Even the people you meet may be drawn to you by your thoughts, including, as I have said before, people from the spirit world. If you think what may be considered "good" positive thoughts, this will attract equally good-minded spirit people. If your thoughts are fearful, depressive and negative, you may attract those of like mind on earth and from the spirit world.

It is therefore worthwhile to try and think in a positive way at all times. I recognise that this is not always easy because the media do tend to bombard us with so much miserable and negative news that it could depress the world's greatest optimist. But, armed with the realisation that staying positive is of benefit to you (and those around you), it is a good idea to train oneself to quickly concentrate on the positive aspects of life. For example, by reminding yourself that you are an eternal spirit being who comes from and will one day return to a loving realm of light. (It may also help to avoid watching TV news and reading the daily newspapers).

When a loved one passes in old age do not be sad, instead think that they are now free from their earthly problems, and in a much brighter, happier place. Say a prayer, wishing them well in their new life.

If you lose your job try to consider that the new challenges will bring you greater knowledge and the chance to make new friends. Everything on earth is temporary.

When you hear of the reported tragedies of the world, remember again, that nobody has or ever will truly die, all are learning through experiences. They may not be very pleasant experiences, but you cannot judge why they may be necessary to the individuals. So be positive, and look for the positive in all things.

Positive thinking is also beneficial to health (although it may not prevent karmic issues); whereas negative thoughts create a vibration that is disharmonious to the mental and emotional bodies (which are within your aura). They therefore create disharmony which can later manifest in the physical body in the form of ill health. Therefore, be positive, stay cheerful and laugh at life as much as you can – remember, it is a temporary, if challenging, spirit adventure.

Train yourself to look for the positive in all aspects of life, for by so doing you will gain the benefit of greater contentment. Your life will also more easily follow the direction and promptings of your spirit.

33. How important is quality of life?

Quality is often an inner experience. A life filled with possessions does not guarantee quality. Whereas a caring, sharing life in which you help others brings an inner sense of quality, happiness, contentment, peace and love to the soul. Many people who live even the most basic of lives in less developed countries are still able to find such a level of quality.

They find moments and degrees of happiness that far exceed many who live comparative lives of luxury. It can be seen that some people who own a big house, a new top of the range car, and expensive electrical luxuries remain quite miserable inside of themselves. Many so called celebrities have pressed the self-destruct button.

Other people become enslaved to their possessions and some continually seek ways in which financially they can become ever wealthier. They may also seek 'power,' to climb to the top of their mountain of 'success.' Perhaps they think people will admire or effectively worship them and that this will make them feel important and happy? Yet it doesn't.

True quality is often experienced in the simple things of life – a walk in a beautiful garden on a sunny day, for instance. Being able to appreciate an inspiring and uplifting arrangement of music gives quality to others. What brings happiness to your soul?

It is indeed the things that bring happiness to each individual, with contentment and peace of mind that I would equate with quality, and this differs between people.

Money to pay for essential services and supplies, for rent or a mortgage and so forth helps. Yet many people have all that they require in this way and still lack genuine quality of life.

The elusive missing ingredient, preventing peaceful contentment, is knowledge of their true spirit nature, their connection with the higher life. Without this they will always be searching for something.

Quality of life improves when the spiritual nature is acknowledged and is expressed in life. It will not take away experiences that you are here to undergo, but it will make it easier for you to understand why certain experiences are necessary.

Live life as you would have wished as a child, expressing and sharing love with all. Help others, with fair reason to your own needs, strive to be happy. Then you will find true quality of life, and when you do return to the spirit world, you will know how wise you have been.

34. Is there life on other planets?

The whole of creation is teeming with life and every planet contains life, even if at the microscopic or mineral level.

Every year, worldwide, there are many thousands of reported UFO sightings. This is a gentle form of communication, gradually allowing people to become aware of, and to accept life elsewhere.

Personally, I do not believe that the beings who come to observe and in some cases interact with us are to be feared. Although, the fact that through ignorance some people might panic if they were to land in an open manner, probably prevents them from doing so at this present moment in time.

When enough of the population of the earth are ready, I believe they will make themselves more openly known to the general public, and that they will be able to help humanity live a more enlightened life.

Furthermore, since you are a spirit being, it is quite possible that in other lifetimes you have lived on other planets; also, that you may do so at some point in your eternal future.

Chapter Seven

Opening the Mind

Question 35

---

35. Final thoughts?

At the beginning of this book I said that my wish was to provide you with easy to follow answers. I hope and trust that this has been the case, and that although this book may appear short in its number of pages, it will feel to you, large in content.

I believe that I have covered most of the basic questions, and perhaps expanded beyond, into areas that will be of interest to you. If you do find further questions formulating in your mind, I do have other books that may answer these for you.

To end this book, I will give you a final and hopefully mind expanding truth and question. It is to say that *all* life is interconnected and is about soul growth. Progression of spirit starts at the microscopic level and slowly develops and advances over aeons of time to reach where you are now. So where will you, the eternal soul being, arrive in another million years and beyond?

Happy seeking...

Recommended Reading

I mention just a few books below; you will find many more listed at my website.

If you seek further proof of the spiritual nature of life, including scientific research and discoveries, near-death experiences, and more, then the Victor and Wendy Zammit book mentioned below is worth reading, it is titled:

A Lawyer Presents the Evidence for the Afterlife

Another book of value, which includes many personal experiences of the author, is by my friend, Brian Sadler, it is:

The Meaning and Purpose of Life

Some of the most informative spirit teaching books, channelled by Robert Goodwin, contain the teachings of White Feather, these include:

Truth from the White Brotherhood
The Golden Thread
Answers for an Enquiring Mind
In the Presence of White Feather
The Enlightened Soul
Wisdom of White Feather

Two books I find most informative contain deep hypnosis case studies of life between lives, by Michael Newton, they are:

Journey of Souls
Destiny of Souls

Made in the USA
Charleston, SC
23 April 2014